salmonpoetry

Until You Make the Shore

Cameron Conaway

Foreword by Playwright Brad Fraser

Published in 2014 by
Salmon Poetry
Cliffs of Moher, County Clare, Ireland
Website: www.salmonpoetry.com
Email: info@salmonpoetry.com

ISBN 978-1-908836-67-0

COVER ARTWORK: Clark Little – ClarkLittlePhotography.com
COVER DESIGN & TYPESETTING: *Siobhán Hutson*
Printed in Ireland by Sprint Print

To Madeline Kiser

3

shayla

Acknowledgments

Grateful acknowledgment is made to the editors of publications in which poems, or versions of them, first appeared:

Bare Root Review of Southwest Minnesota State University
Bijou Poetry Review
Falling Star Magazine
FictionWeek Literary Review
J Journal of CUNY's John Jay College of Criminal Justice
Pocket Change
The Rectangle: The Literary Journal of Sigma Tau Delta
Toe Tree Journal
Turbulence Magazine
Turning the Tide: Journal of Anti-Racist Activism, Research & Education

Special thanks to Penn State Altoona's English and Criminal Justice departments, and to Ander Monson and Richard Siken of the University of Arizona.

Contents

Foreword

These are amazing times we live in. Our perceptions of time, space and intimacy have been changed by the power of instant messaging, email, Skyping and social networking sites. We interact with other human beings, all over the globe, in new and unexpected ways.

I have never actually met Cameron Conaway. He "friended" me on Facebook several years ago. I accepted him as a friend because his Facebook page was, as he himself would turn out to be, filled with fascinating dichotomies; the most obvious being that he has been an MMA fighter and is also a poet. He's not your typical idea of a poet, which works fine for me as I'm not your typical reader of poetry.

This interest led to a correspondence, a long-distance friendship and a number of lengthy phone calls discussing favored authors, the similarities in our less-than-ideal childhoods, and what it means to be a writer.

Somewhere in the midst of all that Cameron tells me he has a book of poetry he'd like me to read. I beg off. Poetry's not really my thing as I'm much more of a dramatist, a "give me characters and a narrative" kind of guy. But as Cameron described what he'd written and why, I finally relented and agreed to look it over. I'm glad I did.

Until You Make the Shore is a series of fictionalized and interlocking poems being narrated by four teen-aged females incarcerated in the Pima County Juvenile Detention Center (PCJDC) in Tucson, Arizona. The author occasionally inserts himself into the work in his role as observer and teacher, but most poems come from a specific character with a very specific history and narrative. Many of the poems seem to be snatches of conversation, bits of internal monologues and other musings.

As one might expect there is a great deal of righteous anger here but there's also a great deal of humanity, a surprising dollop of humour and a more than intermittent flash of hope. These young women are all very interesting characters and the stories they don't so much tell as speak around or allude to are filled with details about family, environment and life that repeatedly score with the reader by being individual and completely convincing. This collection spoke to me in the same way a lot of really good plays can speak to me, through a group of fascinating characters who had affecting stories to tell. I knew I was reading poetry but somehow felt as if I was reading drama as well.

Equally fascinating as the language in this book is the space between the language. There are gaps between words, odd placement to some of the lines and brave spaces of white occupying the largest part of certain pages to indicate lapses or alternations in thought and speech. As a man who's made his living writing dialogue for all sorts of media I know well how the most difficult thing for the writer to indicate, for actors or the reader, are those spaces in communication where nothing is being said. In the theatre it's often indicated by the words BEAT or PAUSE. In film or television the writer devises a bit of business or the description of a changing facial expression to indicate the character has something happening internally that can't really be expressed externally through words; things like allowing a thought to be processed, a decision to be made, searching for the next word or phrase, trying to suppress a sudden urge to do something emotional or physical or even those strange "white noise" moments we can have in our brain when we can't really explain what's been going on in our head at all. In a normal conversation these moments can last anywhere from a nanosecond to several long minutes.

The need for theatrical compression truncates these moments in art but they are still crucially important in any convincing exchange of contemporary dialogue and this is particularly true for people who end up in the penal system who are, often, not quite as articulate and glib as those who write plays or poetry. With Conaway's visual work on the page, as well as the punctuation that evolves as the book progresses, the reader is not just given a story, they're given a very strong sense of how the audio delivery of that story takes place, the rhythm and thought process behind the story. There are points where I feel the reader's thoughts rushing in to fill the voids between text entries are very close to what the character's thoughts were as the story was being related. It's an effect of such brilliance in its subtlety that most people won't even register it's happening—which is exactly how these kinds of things work best.

In reading this book I have to admit that I see Cameron Conaway not just as a promising poet but as a writer of any kind filled with amazing potential. Although I know his other published work is a memoir I also see the origins of screenplays, novels and perhaps even stage plays in his writing. The voices he's dealing with in this work are often savage but the writer still manages to find the beauty and fragility behind the homicidal self-protection. If there's one thing that's made clear about Conaway by his writing and his life, it's that he embraces the antipodean elements of himself, his work and mankind with an openness and willingness that will reward those of us who read him for the rest of his sure-to-be-lengthy and impressive career. I count myself lucky to now be one of those people.

BRAD FRASER is the author of award winning plays including *Unidentified Human Remains and the True Nature of Love*, *Poor Super Man*, *True Love Lies* and many others. His films include *Leaving Metropolis* and *Love and Human Remains* and he was a writer/coordinating producer on Showtime's *Queer As Folk* for the final three seasons of the show. Visit BradFraser.net for more information.

Introduction

The following poems and the characters inhabiting them are imagined, but inspired by experiences teaching creative writing in Pima County Juvenile Detention Center's all-female pod in Tucson, Arizona. A major theme was to lead students to cultivate trust, empathy and knowledge from the often discomforting soil of their past.

The PCJDC's Restorative Justice Model serves as this book's bones. It views youth holistically and has reduced recidivism rates to fifty percent.

Depending on age, court factors, crime committed, conduct and development, a juvenile may stay from a few hours to a full year.

*

U.S. CRIMINAL JUSTICE SYSTEM INFORMATION:

For the first time in history, more than one in one-hundred American adults are behind bars. Parents.

Ninety-three percent are male. Fathers.

Over the past two decades, the percentage of incarcerated women doubled. Mothers.

There is a lack of community awareness, resources and post-sentence programs for females.

Due to overcrowding, inmates are often given a few dollars before they are released at midnight (to avoid media coverage) into the streets.

About PCJDC

One-hundred-eighty-six-bed state-of-the-
ark detention facility. Opened
February two-thousand. Age eight to
seventeen. Uniform colors-conduct
match - green is best, white worst. May check out six
books at one time. Seven-thousand titles
to choose. No shoes, staples, hardcovers, string,
caffeine. Average stay - two weeks. Each youth,
one mentor, one room, one bed, two sandals,
three meals, time. Fifty-five percent are His-
panic/Latino. Court Alternative
Program of Education (CAPE) nine to
four - math, reading, writing, typing, Phys Ed,
rules, nails, numbers, noises, clocks, thoughts, ceilings.

Stat

"Nothing superlative or enchanting should be easily accessible."
WALLACE STEGNER
Where the Bluebird Sings to the Lemonade Springs

Numbers and bars   in a chart

can't speak

like black numbers

on bleached uniforms

on human bodies   or

like the bars that house.

Three or four can't speak

like a forehead crease

nor can a bar chart

chart a scar's story.

They speak to some though.

Those that won't

listen to the dilated pupils of eyes

to the deflated pupils

in their community, walking their streets,

sharing the same blue or gray

or black skies.

The hawks, he thought…

ERNEST HEMINGWAY, *The Old Man and the Sea*

Hawk –
to raise by trying to clear the throat

Merriam-Webster Dictionary

Level 1 - Stabilizer

All newly detained youths will begin at this level. The youth will spend a minimum of three days on this level. They must successfully complete the Stabilization Packet, the Detention Orientation Test, and the Interview Process before they are considered for advancement to the next level.

Graciela

ONE

This other story always makes me laugh now, so here goes, I said. Pennsylvania winter, I'm talking snow everywhere. Sister throwing up in Alf garbage can, mom's mascara tears drip-drop because Penelec turned the heat off——

[Two guards support her weight, guide her past the twenty circled class chairs and into a cell. Two girls call out:] Graciela. Hey Graciela. [No response. Hand raised:] Yes?

Well what about your dad?

Been gone eight years at this point. So they put this metal lock the size of a cowboy hat over the heating unit so you can't get to it---

For real? Shit.

Yup, that's how they do it. It's like the boot they put on cars if you ever saw someone have too many unpaid fines. But anyway, did you know it's a felony to take that thing off the heating unit?

Really?

Did you?

With a hammer. [From her cell:]

in the mirror i stood alive to brush my teeth i cried the mirror dripped ran

[Three times her knuckles knock steel.]

settled in sink i turned the water on to rinse it down to cut the mirror made it faster alive made it leap from the sink to my neck to my neck crawl step by step centipede the ceiling reach the light to wind hook fix itself lift my feet into mouth air swallow off pillow fucking pills

TWO

Poster in pod:

A bridge with a waterfall in the background.

Reads:

COMMUNICATION

An open mind and free dialogue will strengthen the bridges that unify us.

Penciled in the bottom right corner, eraser-smudged:

break out before they break you

THREE

nobody knows about   themselves
            everybody   worries   about
everybody else   people think we are society's
        bad-tasting soup   we are cold soup

soup that needs a stove and stirring   they need
to see things differently

Like what? When you say "things" what do you mean exac––

        all things   like

        the night
who's to say it's not the moon's day
        and disease

                        think of it as dis-ease
and what you have seems
easy
        seems   temporary   a period without freedom is all   and
that ain't so bad now is it

Thought that evening:

knowledge has no ledge.

FOUR

look tattoo tears have different meanings man

you got these cats   on TV talking how
          it means a loved one died and that's it it's like

damn they have this criminology degree   so they know
but they make us seem simple as a garden hose   shit ain't like that

we got people with that tat cause they took life
          wanted that cat's wife to see that fake tear so it killed
her in a different way
people got it half-filled but ain't no such thing as half-killed
means someone killed their loved one

they killed the person that killed their loved one
they halfway there
other half won't fill til they die   rise into the sky

and while they floating   the tear tattoo will drip off
into the soil
into the body in hopes that moisture
clogs the next shotty with love

          sometimes

          people get them for looks like   if you got that tattoo it means
you don't cry for real
and you got a heart of steel so if people blaze you with metal it won't
phase you

          lip tattoo   they say we just

wants to be different and   maybe for some that's true but
what i tell you
     is that if you
look at white people   your people   they get someone they love
tattooed

        on their arm right but if you pull that then get capped
that name gonna be tracked down and now they at risk   we love
people too

but we gots to be careful bout how we show it in public
now ain't no degree tell you that
     i'd like to tell them people to close their books
open their goddamn minds up

     for real their shit's too so-phist-i-cated

some guys i know up in state say they'll write
a woman's name on their wifebeater what they tell you about that

Never said anyth——

guess

A name of someone they love on the outs——

     there you go again

people like you
     think you're so much smarter   if you guess and address
deep shit
it can't be true   cause we're all dumber than a dollar bill uh huh

it's a code letting people know
they're gay   other people do it so the gays stay away

so many groups
so many signs   it's like calculus trying to calculate
what means what and who likes it in the butt

look around a sec see some of these girls and their hair seems wet

     means they down with the puss
outside people think it's all the butch cut

     dude on the news said what happens on the outside

is the same shit that's goin on in the inside
     tell this dude
sometimes shit's the exact opposite   he's not accurate
     but they have to get

our codes cracked

     he said the real world
when talking about the outs   sometimes this house
is realer than the real world

people all smiles walking to their mailbox
waving to neighbors like   hello kyle

but maybe kyle just beat his kid til he hurled
     or is cheating on his wife with young girls I mean young girls

people go in to the grocery store and a woman is all like excuse
     me mam and an old lady is all like awe what a gentle soul
but that woman is getting products from the shelves so she can
     make meth then she sells it to a guy that sells it to kids

     most times people here tell what the fuck they did
sometimes why they did it
     we hide things   we're liable   but in the real world

shit's as real as the bible

FIVE

i fuckin hate when you come in here
with your skin all tanned
i'm mexican
and my shit's as pasty as a white bitches

i need to get the fuck out of here

i'm turning the color you are
or should be   i know you done did
one two three four five crimes

but you're a cracker jack
plus a guy so they ain't gonna

they ain't gonna throw you down
feel you up
wrap and grab your hands and feet
til they bring you here

you're my color
you took it
now I'm takin it

SIX

most girls here see mom or dad dead

    in pics from pigs to identify identity   realness
mom's body   tree limb
dad's face condom wrappers   coffee filters
one girl said whoever suffocated mom nicked

initials in her neck   looked like CKM

so from our cells we all
                yelled across the hall what CKM might mean
came to can't kill me

her mother said can't nobody kill

    life
    only change its shape

we all live
          in   other
or air or dirt

    this girl cried a lot   crying here
no matter
you're a weak ass bitch   can't kill me
let her live life

    bitchless   I pulled the gold

metal from my pencil one time you came in
and weren't looking
          gave it to her
to put CKM on

        in

                    her skin   remind her

she cut it deep in her wrist   CO thought
she cut herself   she did
i mean she didn't

        for good

        not bad

*Do you see pain as opportunity? Some creative writing professors ask
students to write self-obituaries and find that students often avoid
writing of themselves and end up writing about someone else. I'm not
sure if it's because we humans are all connected or because we are, like
you said, wea—*

pops was in vietnam

        only made me touch him when he was drinking
      i think most are weak ass bitches
big deal they see pictures

              they wasn't there mixing spit
with gun powder
      staring through the scope
yelling through the barrel

for pops to take the gun out their mouth

        he'd rock it back and forth like and smile

questions like

how deep can you go
what does it taste like

how does it feel
do you like that you know stupid shit and i couldn't talk so
i'd go like this (nods)

i hated that gun
    when it touched my throat
    when it touched my teeth   gave my shivers

so dad gave it to me
said put it in his mouth now
       i nodded no cause i forgot i could talk now

he said damnit graciela you never f'n listen

    he got up all mad and we had black bean soup cans all
over the floor
and he kicked them screaming about how bad i was'n

how i'd never make it
in war'n
how i didn't care about him like a daughter's supposed to

    he ran to the bathroom kicking cans

and the bang rang my ears

at first i thought dad was just shooting
like he does
you ever been close to a gun shot

not that clo--

it's like you can't help

   but blink

   get away

our trailer was small   kitchen was farthest

i crawled in the cupboard
   got all curled in a ball cause
when he shoots he shoots til he's gone

out of bullets   not just one   and it was

quiet i'm thirteen   it was quiet
i was thirteen

     so after a while

i cracked
open the door and dad was on the floor
   and i couldn't move then

i went to that gas station then
i mean   i'm not saying i had it the worst you be the
judge
but i was actually there when pops lit himself up
i didn't see it but it was better than a picture

i mean

not betterharder

SEVEN

My ass stung
like the bottom
of a stove top pot.
Middle of the yard,
drawers dropped,
his hand,
the whip of a lizard's tail.
I wonder if it hurt
him as much as the pot.

EIGHT

Is there hope? What I mean is, tell me if you think there is something bet—

yeah shit i hope for hope   give me a minute   yeah so i know there's
hope
        cause when i blow my nose i see black
butterflies

        you ever see black butterflies me neither
   another one of god's plans you know
telling black people they'll never be free

        i saved that tissue though want to see it me neither
gives me hope though   god may have a plan for me but i have one
for him

   now you want to know what i do in here i don't know a couple times
       a week

when yall come and teach us poetry and we get pencils i break out

   the lead   hide it in the velcro of my sandals see here
       and i snort it
not for real though you know

   just a little bit cause i swallowed it
   once and coughed at court
while they were yapping about *quid pro quo*   i swear their orange juice
   tasted like i was drinking

silverware but i still snort
just a little so it's in my nose right

then i'll blow

to make new   butterflies

        fuck there's hope   yeah
sometimes you gotta make it though
          sometimes it'll get down stuck in your throat and hurt

NINE

Poster at a commercial gym:

Everyday you are not lifting…THEY ARE.

Pictured:

Three black inmates deadlifting out
* in the yard*
* in orange jumpsuit pants, white wifebeaters.*
Forearms like twisted ropes.

Two black inmates bench pressing out
* in the yard*
* in orange jumpsuit pants, white wifebeaters.*
Triceps like horseshoes.

Level 2 - Recognizer

The youth will participate in all scheduled activities. The youth will spend a minimum of five days on this level. They must successfully complete the Recognition Packet, the Restorative Justice Test, and the Interview Process before they are considered for advancement to the next level.

Eva

ONE

those two moves you showed   triangle choke   right?
   and gogo   gogoplata   they look cool and all
but i ain't never   gonna pull that off on the streets

   because streets have uncountable gravel
you have a mat

   streets have knives
you have two gloves

   streets have eyes from all sides
you have one pair

and besides if i tried it
   that gravel'd stick in my back
make me bleed

   and it'd burn like busted heat
in the shower   it'd probably leave scars
   or something   and people'd ask

how it happen   or if i was born that way
   or if i was whipped at home

i mean   i wouldn't   feel sexy

scars are cool on the front you know

   but back scars mean you done
had it handed to you
   front scars mean you done took it lookin.

TWO

Eva, do you see the world differently because of your time in here?

i made a song and memorized it, shh. can you come closer?

Of course.

k. *(Starts bobbing head)*

i see the world as even
and odd.

thirty-two to chow hall
sixteen to basketball
eleven to library

eight maids afucking
five golden rings

four from door to window
three from door to pee
two from bed to door

and a cartridge in a glock twenty-three.

THREE

last night, i think i bawled
while i slept   last night
i smoothed my two palms

over the two steel beam   grooves
along the wall

beside my bed   in
tune to tupac's changes

until my hands were raw like mi madre's

when i found her in
the tub. I wish
I could see her

hands again to count

the wrinkles the water made

to see   if it is close to my age.

FOUR

when i go

two

i breathe   the smell

deeply in my nose   ugh   to try to filter

    small cells
stalls ten feet apart
    i want privacy   don't want

other girls
knowing what i do when i do it

i don't know why
          i tell you this stuff

usually i cry
      when you leave

     it feels good
     to write or talk about this stupid stuff

last week   when i told you i cut

    mom when   where   she was pregnant
that's one thing
    but this   it's silly isn't it?

do people talk like this on the outs?

    here tears come
here i go again   i like pussy   i like pussy did i tell you that?

I'm sorry cameron i'm sorry i'm sorry.

FIVE

I want everyone to write about a time of pain in your life. There's no need to share, these can all remain anonymous. I want us to try to find how our past shapes us.

[Poem folded matchbox-size and handed to me after class.]

> *"Sometimes you just get so tired of being tired and*
> *you just need to sleep. I'm sorry Eva."*
> ——message on papa's suicide note twenty-six May 2006

newspapers, tv dinners
burnt spoons, chandelier

cobwebs
decorate the trailer, collect
smells of dog shit

    of burnt beef

embalm.

there he is.

    slouched
on the couch watching seinfeld
without eyes.

single-shot shotgun
    in his hands

a remote control.

maggots and blood

    the rice pilaf he'd make

filling the bone bowls
    of his split skull.

SIX

Today we're lucky enough to have Democrat and Republican representatives here to field some questions you may have about John McCain and Barack—

Staff member whispers in my ear:

Take off your hoodie, we're not allowed logos.

It's Penn State Altoona, I wouldn't be here without—

I know, I know—

If it were a marijuana leaf or—

It's the rules. Don't get us in trouble.

SEVEN

With his right hand
he grabbed the eraser—
and I knew
he was about to remove
what I wrote on the chalkboard

Like the tide pulls the words
of others into itself
the eraser took what was mine

So maybe it was just
Key Facts About Aristotle
I still felt the vein
in my forehead appear

EIGHT

last friday   you asked how our past

    shaped us   i been thinking
can you come closer

one thing i took

    stole when mom kicked me out
while she was on parole was three photo albums
now she don't know

i hated her

she hated me

      but i wanted those memories
i got pictures in my pocket
cute right?

see the sequins on my socks?

    on the streets when i be touchin cats i'd tape

a knife to those same socks with part of the handle out
so i could take a stand and demand to get licked

this one on the high-chair

    mom said big brother'd always put the pacifier
back in my mouth when i spit it out
can you come a little closer

i deep-throat dick with these same lips

god damnit

motherfuckers never paid up   i just

when you told us to think other girls

said they done
        lived hard lives
    they tougher   now than then

none said if they better or not

i'm not better   man   i don't know
what you wanted from the assignment

but i sure as hell ain't better   maybe just thinking

makes me feel like i'm not better   is that

what you wanted?

What I wanted:

What she gave.

Reflection not reflect-shun.

NINE

cameron, *[motions me to come closer]* my boyfriend bo wrote
me a poem *[from over her shoulder I read]*

if the moon were an eye
and i could be the moon
i would watch you

through beige curtains
all night while you slept

cause i would never
need to sleep

only change perspectives
and so see you from infinite angles
and so see you in a way

i haven't before.
if the moon were an eye
and i could be the moon.

TEN

So, tell me about your man Bo.

I loved him since
I was eleven

I love him
eleven

I love him
eleven

funny huh?

*Love that wordplay, you're starting to see! So besides letters, how
else do you keep in touch? Are you allowed to call or have him
visit?*

besides letters? numbers   *[a smile starts, she hides it by looking at
the floor]*
well, like last night

on my back

in my bed

   i traced bo's name
in the air   until
i could no longer

feel
but i kept my eyes open   when my fingers tingled

i could see
streaks of red   my hand a wand

fourth of july
swirling sparklers in the backyard

dogs barking, burgers on the grill.
i like the ones with deep grill marks
                       the ones burned a little bit.

ELEVEN

hey cameron, you know when I get out?

When?

i'm asking you.

I'm not sure.

i'm scared these nights alone
    my mind

zones out   i don't know how

goneness   separateness

can't shake it

    same place
they took turns with me   alley of cici's pizza
    on my break

i'll wake
swear my sweat smells like the pepsi they poured over me

my sheets
     street gasoline and tucson sun steamed cat pee

i hurt down there, cameron
i'm doing what they did
in my sleep   i can't

take this shit and sweep it clean

the way the c.o.'s rush in when I dream
the way they rush in loud, swarm, surround

Level 3 - Assessor

At this level, the youth will prepare for developing a Relapse Prevention Plan. The youth will remain a minimum of three days on this level. They must successfully complete the Assessing Packet and demonstrate an understanding of the five life skills during the Interview Process before they are considered for advancement to the next level.

Precious

ONE

Last week we talked about descriptive writing and enjambment. Enjambment comes from a French word meaning… Anyone?

Straddle! *[Laughter breaks out]*

Right! And why?

The poetry straddles two lines, like one goes into the other.

Yes! You guys are spot on this week.

Girls!

Girls, yes. You girls are spot on this week. I asked everyone to have an example for me, remember? Something that used enjambment to say something unexpected, right? Any volunteers?   Nobody?

Go for it Precious.

[More laughter. She unfolds her paper, postures, clears her throat.]

Mi tía es como a teddy bear…

[She pauses. Silence. I cough. Then:]

cholla!

TWO

Found crinkled after class

Description lesson for Cameron

<u>Precious</u> <u>Toro</u>

Thirteen

Five feet one inch
One-hundred and ten pounds

Tohono O'odham

<u>My room at home</u>

JT and Jonas posters
O'odham maze on ceiling above bed

pink blankets
many pillows four or five maybe

two windows
light brown carpet, scratchy

dirty clothes on floor (mom yells at me)
~~plastic baggie in bed~~

white hairs from puppy Chloe
small TV it is black

flower vase has four fake roses
two Yankee Candles – Home Sweet Home and Garden Sweet
Pea (best kind!)

radio alarm clock and lamp on dresser
straightener and blow dryer by outlet

please tell me if this is right or wrong

THREE

Precious, you've been here how long now?

Twenty-six days

What do you miss the most?

I miss
            handles –

on doors, toilets, cups, garbage cans, jean zippers, showers,
cereal boxes.

Getting lost in the fields
on the back of a shredded wheat box.

        Using my hands   to pull, push, pry.

It's all automatic now, or it slides.

Look at these hands –

    they made for QVC.
Street dreams aren't made of these.

FOUR

Precious, what did it mean to you when she called you a "hardened criminal?"

Dreams are soft, Cameron.   My uncle's

knuckles are vapor in dreams.   My throat

    doesn't burn when I scream,
even a falcon's talons can't hurt me   but reality

    is abrasive   concrete pebble-izes knee skin

      when we fall
in love it feels good or it hurts   so I guess

                she meant   I don't dream enough?

FIVE

I spent the day digging

    staples out of spirit & life:

a magazine

from the benedictine sisters of perpetual adoration

    for the girls in detention

stories of iona pilgrimages

dreams
            reality

their dreams

        crave normalcy

not

        licking snicker wrappers from roads

calories for a baby   *created*

    by violence   *created*

by a serrated knife

            carving   *shaping*

the inside of cheek   *to force a fake*

smile and moan

the inside of vagina   to force a fake

lubrication

their reality   is as staples

                              burnt then cast

        their spirit

flashbacks to forceful penetration   and

        shanks for mutilation

        their life   stripping

the paint of four white walls and the floor
                              or
                              the flesh of whoever steps to this

SIX

For our theme today, Crimes are not our Sum: On being publicly defined by a single moment, we've brought in players from the women's wheelchair basketball –

[Staff member to newspaper reporter with a camera:]

Make sure not to get their faces, just ponytails and backs and stuff.

SEVEN

You remember   when I told you I

     punched that little girl

in the mouth
          for her
Halloween basket?   You remember?

     Well I smiled when I said it
and I didn't mean it. I mean I been

crying a lot   about why I smiled
if something is wrong with me

I liked how her blood in the darkness

was black   could have been a shadow

brought down from leaves   I mean

I don't know
if I'da saw her blood   the red

I hope I wouldn't have smiled

   I bleed   you know

red
same as her

we are more we are the same like

   I only thought about
how she was probably rich

and I was definitely hungry
and I hit her real hard

even when she was done

I hit her
till she stopped crying

and moving. I cry cause I don't know
if she was playin   dead for me to stop

or

I just don't know why I smiled

or hit her

again

once or twice was enough.

EIGHT

Here's a poem I wrote with a simile like you said. I got both like and as in there.

Bars bang loud   rattle.

Sound moves
as smoke,

waves as myself

      six months ago.
Reminds me   what begins loud

      fades like the so black it's blue of one

raven in the brown Rez desert.

NINE

"The only time I'll sign the roman numerals after my name is at the bank so he can't take my money."

unwrapping him
I saw the tip of his rubbery
green tail poking through the altoona mirror:
pages filled with killings or cocaine
or baseball   and my brown eyes
and the motion sensitive
red of his lit up when we saw each other
I pressed his chiseled body
to my chest   said something about mothra
or mama   fiddled with the proper way to plunge
batteries into his ass because I never wanted
him to look at me
with bloodshot eyes
I untucked myself, sidled
night after night down the sides
of the steps so they wouldn't creak
to place him   and his enemy with a similar
name   mechagodzilla   across the silver strip
that separated
our kitchen from that room
their prerecorded roars would wake me
in case somebody broke-in
or tried to leave

TEN

You been here, what, about a month?

Thirty-six days. How many rounds are in
boxing matches?

Twelve.

How many minutes in
a round?

Three.

Twelve times three is thirty-six.

Yup.

How many rounds have I been in here?

*I don't know. Is there anything you personally do to try to keep in
touch with the outs?*

    Sometimes I think

I got the style of a stillborn child –
but when they cut the lights at nine

    passing cars are waves,

sirens are seagulls,

    the wall is my man's back and I'm rubbing lotion.

The C.O.'s sixteen steps are a beating
    flag from the ocean winds.

You ever listen to Mobb Deep's Quiet Storm?

You know it.

ELEVEN

[as I'm leaving:]

Cameron, I get out tomorrow

you did not stay long

[thoughts: but it is rougher where you are going]

five years later on tucson nightly news:

former juvenile offender

graduates

from pima community college

with her associates degree

in nursing

cap and gown

exchanged

for handcuffs

pleads guilty to possession

and distribution of cocaine

tune in tomorrow night

for an in-depth look

at the first of our four-part series:

the making of a criminal

Level 4 - Planner

The youth will continue to participate in all scheduled activities. The youth is expected to conduct peer-teaching of the Orientation Process and the Restorative Justice Model. In order to ensure an understanding of the Restorative Justice Model, the youth will be required to write an essay on "What Restorative Justice Means to Me."

Arianna

ONE

*Arianna, I'm here so infrequently and, honestly, the appearance in here
startles me when I walk in. What does it look like to you?*

Clean.

Crack everywhere back home

    no need to worry where I step

except if I screw up   and they boot me   then

I get to steppin is that good?

Can you tell me more?

    Look, I climbed the ladder

like a soldier   a woman warrior   check it:

when I got here I was Level 1 Stabilizer   means

    time to detox and think about my slipping

the community came when I moved to Level 2 Assessor

    got to wear these sandals and a green shirt instead of white

and learn so I'm better equipped to handle fights

then I moved to Level 3 Recognizer   means

   I got to eat out   away

from my cell   from my toilet   see the rewards?

   Then I moved to Level 4 Planner and this was the bomb
   dot com

   got to get me a facial

   my nails did

   a later reading time to finish Countee Cullen

   to write poetry

   watch movies on Saturday

   shave on Sunday

far as colors   people on the outs always say it's bare

   but there's color in faces and smiles

                  here and there when people got personality.

TWO

So they call you the Vet in here huh?
What's that in-between stage like?

First, this here's my last time in, you best believe.

Between sentences

    time's pace slows

to think
       or play pickup ball.

    When I'm open

I feel like I could knock it down.

    I raise my hands

and call for the ball   but when it comes

    it's picked

or if I get it I'm stripped

or if I shoot it I'm swatted

or if I shoot it and get hacked there's no free throw

or if I do score there's no and-one.

THREE

I've been here so long I see the world

    in squares and rectangles.

TV during the Cardinals' Superbowl –

    every five yards

a casket   and the endzone

    an end zone.

Close a u or an n   and you have a cell

    and an h   a cell

with a path in   or out

but without.

FOUR

We've written about pain, but now let's switch it up. I want everyone to write a letter—

Can it be a poem?

Yes, write a letter or poem to a loved one. I'll float around and help.

Dear Mama,

I'm in here and you're up there
but just as I was little
we share the same porch
and rocking chair. I recognize
now
your rattling keys that woke me
were more than noises
nuisances
and the birthday balloons
wrapped around prickly pear
were more than for looks
and the bean burritos
were more than for the smell
and the way you scrubbed
the grease from your hands
after work   more   more

so you could run
your fingers through my hair.
So my stomach would be full.
So I knew you loved me.
So you could buy me presents.

I recognize now and
tell me you know I know.

Talk to me
through my new nail polish swirls
or through the sound
of the basketball net
and wink at me
through a C.O.'s eyes
or through the flecks of sun
the clouds make flicker.
Let it be your breath
when the heat kicks on
while the steel doors shut
while the lights cut off.
Let it be your smile in the arc
of the water from the fountain.

FIVE

Arianna, last night was your last night sleeping in PCJDC. What do you think about that?

For the first time in my life   I had fun

   crying.   I cried

                      on my side

til tears filled the swirl   of my ear   then

I switched sides   cried deeper

   to see if   a tear from my left cheek

could keep itself together enough

   to drag   its body   well

the rest of its body

          since part of it was left behind

up and over the protruding part you know

         like that step leading to the ear swirl

it was brighter on that side

          from the moonlight.

Hope to see you someday on the outs, teach.   Peace.

SIX

In the library.

Poster of Denzel Washington states: READ.
He's holding Green Eggs and Ham.
He's smiling.

Poster of Mel Gibson states: READ.
He's holding 1984.
He's not smiling.

SEVEN

thank you for allowing

*me to speak with yall today   it's
been*

*an honor to share my   three darkest
moments   and*

I hope you can see that our past

*is like a difficult to eat fruit   and if
we reflect on those moments*

*and juice them   the insights
we learn*

can nourish us for years to – [led in by two guards]

Arianna?   Hey it's so nice to see

I mean

what happened?

EIGHT

each day   dawn

ice cubes   sink

yellow bus   screech

faucet water   on

warm melts   cold

NINE

We often talk about how good can come from mistakes, or pain. How positive thinking is so powerful. So, I'm going to read a poem I wrote and I want somebody, as soon as I finish, to walk like they imagine the poodle would walk judging by the poem's rhythm.

Ok, White pood—

Wait, you want us to actually get up and walk around when you're done?

Expect might be a better word.

Ready?   [Silence, smiles.]

White poodle. Pink bow on neck. Sidewalk. Owner comes out says Whoa. Owner steps closer to dog says Whooaa. Dog looks back looks back says Nothin. Four legs four legs four legs four. White poodle. Pink bow on neck. Sidewalk. Owner runs. White poodle. Pink bow on neck. Curb. Owner sprints. Owner says Hey. I turn. Not me. Not me he was talking to. Wiffle ball bat to, to leather shoe. White poodle. Pink bow on neck on road I froze. Owner says Nooo. Froze. Stands with hands on head. Beep-beep cars beep-beep. Froze. Minute-silence. Tugs pants stoops down to ground to cradle poodle. White poodle. Pink bow on neck.

[Girls look at each other. Precious prances to the circle's center. Laughter breaks out. Arianna says:]

No, no, no, damn girl. You're hopping like a seagull or some shit, let me drop a dime to you.

NOTE: "drop a dime" means to assist or help

CAMERON CONAWAY, Executive Editor at GoodMenProject.com, was the 2012 Poet-in-Residence at the Mahidol Oxford Tropical Medicine Research Unit in Thailand and the 2007-2009 Poet-in-Residence at the University of Arizona's MFA Creative Writing Program. Conaway is the author of *Caged: Memoirs of a Cage-Fighting Poet* (Threed Press, 2011) and *Bonemeal: Poems* (Finishing Line Press, 2013). He is on the Editorial Board at *Slavery Today: A Multidisciplinary Journal of Human Trafficking Solutions*. Conaway's writing has appeared in *The Guardian, The Huffington Post, ESPN* and *Rattle*. Follow him on Twitter @CameronConaway.